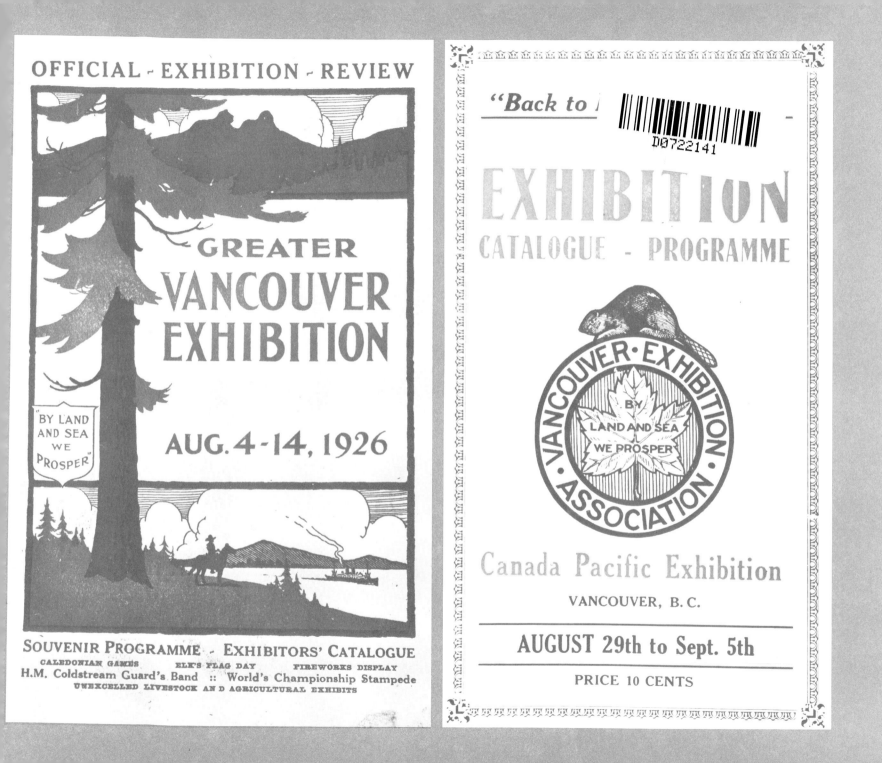

OFFICIAL · EXHIBITION · REVIEW

GREATER VANCOUVER EXHIBITION

"BY LAND AND SEA WE PROSPER"

AUG. 4 - 14, 1926

SOUVENIR PROGRAMME - EXHIBITORS' CATALOGUE

CALEDONIAN GAMES   ELK'S FLAG DAY   FIREWORKS DISPLAY
H.M. Coldstream Guard's Band :: World's Championship Stampede
UNEXCELLED LIVESTOCK AND AGRICULTURAL EXHIBITS

"Back to

D0722141

EXHIBITION
CATALOGUE - PROGRAMME

VANCOUVER · EXHIBITION · ASSOCIATION
BY LAND AND SEA WE PROSPER

Canada Pacific Exhibition

VANCOUVER, B. C.

AUGUST 29th to Sept. 5th

PRICE 10 CENTS

S
557
C22
B74
1982

S

The
Pacific National Exhibition
An Illustrated History

David Breen & Kenneth Coates

University of British Columbia Press

Vancouver

Pacific National Exhibition:
An Illustrated History

Canadian Cataloguing in Publication Data

Breen, David H.
  The Pacific National Exhibition

  ISBN 0-7748-0167-0 (bound)
  ISBN 0-7748-0160-3 (pbk)

  1. Pacific National Exhibition — History — Pictorial works. I.
Coates, Kenneth, 1956-
II. Title
S557.C22V354   607'.34'71133   C82-091211-5

Book Designed by Victoria Farmer
International Standard Book Number 0-7748-0160-3 (pc)
0-7748-0167-0 (hc)
Printed in Canada

Contents

Preface

Fairs! What images they evoke! For most the word brings forth memories of earliest childhood and of youthful adventures on warm summer afternoons. While these images are mainly light and frivolous, fairs are nonetheless part of a heritage going back to the ancient past. In their varied and overlapping forms, fairs, pageants, carnivals, bazaars, and exhibitions have brought people together for centuries — to celebrate, to be informed, and to be entertained. The word fair comes from the Latin *feria*, meaning holiday, and from classical times to the modern day, fairs have been part of a yearly ritual. As such, they offer a marvelous and revealing window through which to view a society at any given time. This is certainly true in the New World, where for two hundred years, whether in the form of small rural gatherings or urban extravaganzas, fairs have been an important feature of North American life. People by the million are drawn to participate in agricultural competitions, to view commercial and industrial displays, or to join the revelry of the carnival.

While they represent one of the most common summer activities on this continent, each fair has its own unique features and characteristics. Three prominent components — agriculture, boosterism and entertainment — can be found in virtually every North American fair. There are, of course, other activities which form an integral part of most fairs including hobby and craft competitions, horticultural shows, presentations of "women's work", athletic events and horse racing. But it is the three key elements or more correctly the balance between them, which determines the structure and content of a particular fair. Each fair has its particular blend of these components and therefore, in many ways reflects the values and aspirations of the community in which it is situated. The fair stands as a statement of how a people perceive their past, present, and future.

This is the story of one fair, Vancouver's Pacific National Exhibition, which has evolved from a small gathering on the forested fringe of the city to its current status as one of the largest events of its type in North America. In a special and important way this is also a story of Vancouver.

The Photographs

As an historical record the photograph stands strikingly apart. Only the camera permits us to see the past as though it were present — the camera enables us to take an instant and fix it for all time. Viewers can look once more at Vancouver's first fair in 1910, at the Fraser Valley Milk Producers Association Booth in 1926, or at the 1954 Opening Ceremonies for the British Empire Games. For this reason the more than 9,000 photographs that comprise the Pacific National Exhibition's picture collection are a treasure of incalculable value. The photographs on the following pages come almost entirely from this source and represent the quality and diversity of the entire collection. To make this outstanding collection more readily available to the public and to ensure its proper preservation, the Pacific National Exhibition has recently presented its picture collection to the Vancouver City Archives.

Acknowledgements

The authors are anxious to acknowledge the very special debt they owe to those mainly unknown persons who for seventy-five years under the auspices of the Vancouver Exhibition Association and later with the Pacific National Exhibition had the wisdom to create and then preserve the photographic record upon which this book is based. We are grateful to Diane Purvey whose competent and congenial assistance helped to bring order to these thousands of unsorted photographs. Our indebtedness extends also to the helpful staff of the Historical Photographs Section at the Vancouver Public Library, and to the archivists at the Vancouver City Archives in whose professional care the P.N.E. papers and photographs now rest.

The Beginning

"In the opinion of this meeting the time has arrived for the establishment of an Exhibition Association for Vancouver to embrace Fat Stock, horses, dogs, poultry, also Horticultural, Agricultural and industrial interests and also for the object of maintaining the City of Vancouver in that leading position she by rights should occupy.**"**

Minutes of Preliminary Meeting, Vancouver Exhibition Association, 31 May 1907

1

First Years, 1907–1919

British Columbia has a long tradition of fairs and exhibitions, dating from a small gathering held near Victoria on Vancouver Island in 1861. Although it was incorporated in 1886, the City of Vancouver was slow to host its own annual fair since many citizens felt that the nearby New Westminster exhibition, started in 1869, was serving the needs of the lower mainland. On 31 May 1907, a dozen Vancouver businessmen gathered in the office of realtor Thomas Duke and resolved to develop a fair for the city. To this end, they organized the Vancouver Exhibition Association, a body comprised of a six–man executive supported by twenty directors.

To manage the fair, the directors established a series of committees to handle the general tasks of finance, works, publicity, and transportation. Preparations for the exhibition itself were delegated to eighteen departments, each responsible for the organization and supervision of its own segment of the larger fair. To staff the numerous departments, the Vancouver Exhibition Association drew largely on outside groups, including agricultural, horticultural, sporting, and social organizations. Preparations went slowly, and the organizers encountered many difficulties; money had to be raised through civic by–law submissions and the sale of memberships, and the chosen site, Hastings Park, on the city's east side, had to be secured for exhibition purposes. By 1910 the directors were ready, necessary facilities were in place, amusement devices had been erected, industrial displays and agricultural competitions were organized, and appropriate dignitaries, including the Prime Minister, Sir Wilfrid Laurier, and Sir Robert Baden Powell, had agreed to grace the proceedings. Vancouver's fair could finally be launched.

The first fairs were organized with one main aim — to promote Vancouver. The presentation was aptly dubbed "The Industrial Exhibition", for the focus was clearly on the industrial and resource potential of the city and its hinterland. The fair grew in popularity over the next decade, although the Vancouver Exhibition Association's decision to continue operating during World War I sparked considerable controversy. Vancouverites flocked to the fair on an annual basis, drawn by the entertainment, the many delights and attractions of the carnival, and by the fact that the exhibition was Vancouver's show, the city's statement to the world of its promise and potential.

Hastings Park In The 1890's

This photo shows the early development of Hastings Park, given to the city by the provincial government in 1889. The first facilities on the site were designed for horse racing, but this picture seems to be of a livestock sale or show rather than a horse race.

2

Hastings Park Racetrack c. 1905
Fans of turf and track travelled out from Vancouver, often by boat, to enjoy a regular schedule of races. The facilities were at best adequate, and the distance from the city to the park meant that crowds were only moderate.

3

Vancouver Exhibition Association: Search for a Home

❝That this meeting is of the opinion that the time has arrived when public opinion should be awakened to the interests they possess in that splendid property — the Hastings Park — which for twenty years has been totally neglected and abandoned by the Park Authorities and has been monopolized by and for racing purposes — that a public meeting should be held in the near future to lay all the facts before the people in order that their rights may be asserted and that the progress of the city may not be arrested.**❞**

Minutes of the Executive Council, V.E.A., 3 July 1908.

J. J. Miller, First President Of The Vancouver Exhibition Association

Although J. C. V. Field Johnson, a newspaperman previously involved with the Winnipeg Exhibition, is credited with providing the impetus which led to the founding of the V.E.A., J. J. Miller soon emerged as the leader of the organization. A real estate agent, Miller served as the President of the exhibition association from 1908 to 1922. Aided by Manager H. S. Rolston, Miller guided Vancouver's fair from a rather shaky beginning to a well–earned status as one of Western Canada's premier urban exhibitions.

Vancouver And Hastings Park, 1910

Since it was located in the northeast corner of the city, Hastings Park (arrow) was removed from the downtown core and existing residential areas. Many people, including several founders of the Vancouver Exhibition Association, saw the establishment of the fair as a means of encouraging development on the east side of Vancouver. The staging of the exhibition had the expected impact, as roads, transit lines, and other civic services were extended towards Hastings Park.

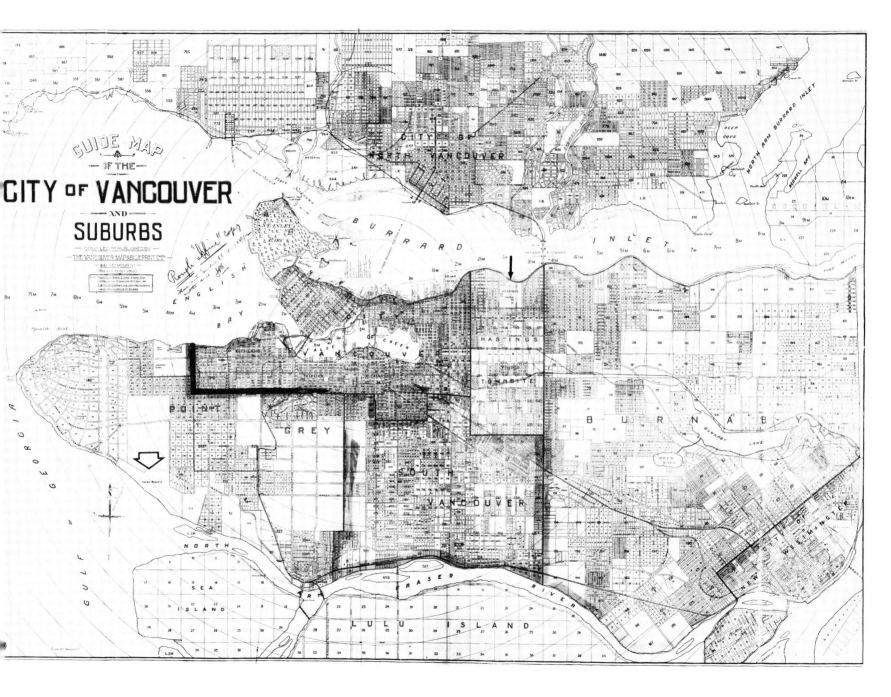

The First Fair: Opening Ceremonies

"Before a crowd of 5,000 people of all ages, sexes and stages in life, Sir Wilfrid Laurier formally opened Vancouver's first exhibition yesterday afternoon. Although the plans for the reception and address of the premier, as arranged by the fair committee, carried out nicely, still a crowd of rowdies, occupying a section of the grandstand, marred the speech of the Liberal leader by their cries of "sit down" and their "rooting" over the harness races which were in progress. A throng of curious people, each striving for a view of the distinguished visitor, surged about the gates leading to the grandstand, causing such a jam that the services of two mounted policemen were required to keep them back. As it was, several ladies of the party were badly shoved about and jammed, and it was only with great difficulty that the police were able to segregate the persons allowed in the boxes from the curious throng that sought admission."

Vancouver *Daily News–Advertiser*, 17 August 1910

Arrival Of Sir Wilfrid Laurier, 1910

To herald the opening of Vancouver's first fair, the association wanted to secure the services of suitable dignitaries. Sir Robert Baden Powell presided over a Boy Scout Jamboree on the first day of the fair. Sir Wilfrid Laurier, Prime Minister of Canada, came to officially open the fair on the second day. His arrival touched off a small riot when crowds attempting to get into the grandstand to hear him speak overwhelmed the ticket takers. By the end of the fair, about 68,000 people had passed through the gates. The 50¢ admission charge remained in effect until the 1960's.

The Booster Spirit

"Never was the spirit of the west, the ready determination to brook no obstacles better shown than in the Hastings Park at the present moment, where, carven out of the heart of the forest wilderness, ready for the most critical inspection of the citizen and visitor, is Vancouver's exhibition and playground, by nature eminently fitted as the most beautiful of its kind in the west, and through the industry and ability of the fair directors and management as perfect in all departments as could be expected for an opening year. First things are crude and rough, lacking the finished polish and machine–like smoothness that years of trial bring, but nevertheless as a lesson of what may be done within a few months when the right men have charge and the right spirit directs the efforts the exhibition this year stands unique. Given by the open hand of nature a ground gently sloping to the green waters of the inlet, protected from fierce winds, but yet open enough for one to gain full glimpses of a smiling British Columbia sky, the various–shaded woods that skirt the tract whereon Vanouver hopes to show its progress and energy to the world, the men who have had the making of the exhibition property have truly done wonders. Where a short while ago there was nothing but the densest of woods defying the hand of man to work a change in their primeval condition now the manufacturers of the east and west, the north and south are displaying their wares in handsome and commodious buildings, live stock of all kinds is on exhibition and crowds of busy, throbbing humanity pour here and there along the 'skid road', the future, perhaps, furthest removed from the first condition of things."

Vancouver *Daily News–Advertiser*, 16 August 1910

Street Cars At The Exhibition Grounds, 1910

When the first fair was held at Hastings Park, the city's street car grid had not been extended that far east. Special arrangements were reached with the B.C. Electric Railway, and a line was opened in time for the exhibition. Access to the grounds was also provided by the C.P.R. train from Vancouver and by boat to the docking facilities available at Brighton Beach.

For the People

"The park will not be merely an exhibition grounds but will be open to the use and enjoyment of the people for the entire year. The gates will be ever open and it will be kept as a beautiful park, such as will be greatly appreciated by the people, particularly those in the Eastern side of the city. These already visit it in great numbers. The Industrial Hall will be used for conventions, exhibitions of different kinds, such as poultry, dog or flower shows. Also for balls and parties and big gatherings and meetings.

Besides the value which the association and the exhibition will be from a commercial standpoint as an advertising medium of the resources of British Columbia to the whole world and its value as a means of encouraging individual enterprises, it will be an excellent avenue for the desires of the people for recreation, pleasure and social intercourse. It will also be a means for the interchange of ideas upon all kinds of subjects and will serve as a great public school in which all may derive some education in the advancement of the world in industrial, commercial, agricultural and scientific matters."

Speech by V.E.A. President J. J. Miller, reported in Vancouver *Daily Province*, 13 August 1910, p. 17.

Industrial Building, 1910

The showpiece of the V.E.A.'s first fair was the Industrial Building, financed through monies received from civic by-laws. This elaborate facility was built with great haste and little caution and soon fell on hard times. The towers proved unstable, and the entire structure deteriorated rapidly. Renamed the Women's Building and relegated to a less prominent role in the fair, the facility was finally demolished in 1936.

The First Exhibition, August 1910

Fall fairs were more common and ideally suited for farmers' participation. The decision to schedule an August fair reflects the greater strength of the horse breeding and racing fraternity and industrial exhibitors.

The First Fair: A Tour Through the Grounds

❝Entering Industrial Hall through the main door at the west end of the building the visitor's attention is first attracted to the circular booth in the center of the open space, lying immediately in front on the center block of stalls. This, together with the west semi–circular end of the main block, is occupied by Little Bros. with a display of candies, staple groceries, toys and notions. To the right, along the side of the building, Hocks and Lovick's fine display of pianos are to be seen. Proceeding down the south aisle, on the right hand side, the magnificent display installed by David Spencer Ltd., attracts the attention and admiration of every person entering the hall. This firm, occupying five stalls, has fitted them up to represent the interior of a modern home, with a bedroom, library, dining room and kitchen. The walls and floors of the stalls are carpeted in a style that would fit the best and most modern of residences, while the fine furniture used in the exhibit attracts the attention of all who view it. On the same side of this aisle, beyond the doorway leading to the veranda, the booth occupied by D. Parry, with a fine display of engravings, is to be seen. Proceeding down the aisle the visitor sees on the same side the stalls of M. J. Foster, the Electric Lace and Silk Company, Harry Wilson & Co.; also those of O. L. Charlton, with a fine display of honey, and the Kelowna Tobacco Company. This concern displays British Columbia tobacco which is rapidly growing in favour.

Turning and proceeding back this aisle, the visitor sees the display of the Thompson Stationery company, in the east semi–circular end of the main block. Here a number of office desks, office furnishings and equipment are on display. The Norris Safe and Lock company, with safes of all sizes, from those weighing a few hundred pounds to the massive affairs weighing several tons, occupy the first booth on the south side of the block. James Stark Ltd. presents a fine exhibit of rattan furniture, rugs and carpets in the next booth, while C. W. Roos and Perry–Gordon company occupy the next two stalls, the latter firm with a display of horse medicines and stock food. Ronald McMaster, with a stall devoted to the Maple Leaf clothes drier, and Mackey, Smith & Blair, with a fine showing of knit goods, come next in the line, while beyond these the Daily Province occupies a stall. The last two booths on the aisle are given over to the exploitations of the goods put out by the Brackman & Ker and the Vancouver Milling companies respectively.

Proceeding around to the north aisle, opposite the display of Hicks and Lovick's, the exhibition and demonstrations of Piper & Co. Ltd. of hot water heaters, furnaces and pumping appurtenances are to be seen. The first booth on the north side of the centre block is occupied by the Electric Water Heater company, where demonstrations of the efficiency of this system are given daily. The next booth is that which houses the display of the Singer Sewing Machine company while the Vancouver Garment company, with an exhibit of Vancouver–made garments and clothes comes next. The next three stalls are given over to the Woodward stores, with a general display of their wares. White and Bindon occupy a small booth with their display of stationery and printing, while next to this is that of the News Advertiser.

The White Sewing Machine agency have the next three stalls, showing everything modern in their line. The next booth, and the last on this block, is that of the British Columbia Electric Company, where there is an office for the convenience of concessionaries, and a fine display of electrical goods is shown.

On the north side of this aisle the first stall is that occupied by W. J. McMillan & Co., with a showing of teas, while the Stien Import Company, with cash registers and safes, comes next. P. R. Cummings, the Burroughs Adding Machine company, H. B. Watts, J. C. Kloepper and Foreman & Armstrong all have exhibits housed in booths along this line. The Electrical Supply company, with a display of chandeliers and other electrical goods, come next, while the Asbestos company, limited, and J. Leckie's fine shoe display finish out the aisle.

At the east end of the building, in the centre space, the British Columbia Sugar Refining company has erected a tasteful booth, showing in it a number of the products of the sugar cane. The displays of the Petrie Manufacturing company and the Westminster Board of Trade are on the south side of the building, while Phillips & Brown, the Crown Broom company, Storey & Campbell and the Park Drive Furniture company all occupy space in this end.

Leaving the main floor, and going by way of the northeast set of stairs to the gallery, the visitor, on alighting on this upper portion of the building is struck by the magnificent display of the Local Council of Women. Fancy work of all kinds, tapestries, embroideries, doilies, sofa cushions, baby goods and such, tastefully arranged in show cases and along counters, tend to make the display of the women one of the best in the Exhibition. Proceeding around the gallery the visitor sees the art exhibit with its fine assortment of paintings, oil and watercolors by local artists. At the end of the building a showcase filled with mounted birds is shown by a local taxidermist, while more pictures and a display of ores finish up the sights in this end. Along the north gallery the work of the school children will create a favourable impression of Vancouver schools in the minds of every visitor who views the display. Several fine examples of furniture made by the pupils of the manual training school shows the efficiency of this department of the schools.

Machinery Hall

Machinery hall, like the larger building, Industrial hall, is also divided into booths, though for the most part all spaces are larger than in the other building. Entering from through the south door, the first exhibit the visitor sees on the left hand side is that of the Walworth Ralston company. Wagons, buggies, light vehicles, cream separators, incubators and dairy supplies form the greater part of the exhibit, though nearly everything necessary to the successful dairy or poultry farm could be found in this space. The booth is walled in by a very artistic wire fence. The next booth, that of E. B. Horsman & Co. contains a fine display of wagons, buggies and farming implements. The Moore Light company, with a display of gas lights and independent gas lighting plants, comes next, while the Vancouver Machinery company's exhibit of gas engines occupies the next stall. Stancliffe & Co., with a display of gas engines, the Fox Gasoline Lighting System and an assortment of wire rope occupy a large booth. The last exhibit on this side of the building is that of E. G. Prior & Co., containing a display of vehicles of all kinds and descriptions. Proceeding back through the building,

the first display on the east side of the structure is that of A. G. Brown & Co., in which farming implements, fine vehicles, gas engines and heavy wagons are shown. G. Blackwell, with a display of steel shingles, occupies the next booth, while Storey & Campbell, with their exhibit of wagons and other vehicles, come next. The Columbian Pulley Manufacturing company occupies the booth next to this, and the fine carriages and wagons of the Dominion Car Company are the next along the aisle. The British Columbia Marine Railway company's display finishes up the exhibits in this building.

To the east of the Machinery hall, lying between the Industrial building and the Skid road, the magnificent garden planted by the Royal Nurseries company attracts a great deal of attention. This display, free from advertising, was installed by the company, and greatly adds to the beauty of the fair grounds.

On The Skid Road

Petrified women, sacrificial crocodiles from the sacred river Ganges; chickens that lay eggs and dusky negroes who dodge swiftly thrown baseballs, to say nothing of the numerous Salome dancers, Spanish Carmens, Dutch comedians and chorus girls, are some of the attractions that are being offered the visitors at the fair this week. Everything new and novel in the amusement line, every means that human mind can devise to gather in the spare nickle, dime or quarter of the amusement seeker, is now in operation.

To do the Skid Road properly would take at least half a day. To witness each show, see all the dancing attractions, throw baseballs at each of the African dodgers, ride the merry–go–rounds and be entertained at the half hundred other resorts, would require a sum of money not less than $5. And to eat a sandwich at each of the stands, drink lemonade at all the booths, or smoke cigars at each tabacconist's stand would require at least another $5 bill.

Most ingenious of all the schemes now in operation is that now doing business on the south road. Here a dusky negro sits on a board fixed to an iron bar, directly over a pool of water. A baseball, thrown at a target above this son of Ham's head, springs a trap, and allows the seat on which the black man sits to move backward, throwing the occupant head-foremost into the water. This device is now one of the most popular on the Road. Not only the person throwing the ball but every one about gets a share of the amusement.

Starting in at the south end of the Road, the first concessionary is a rotund gentleman, who proclaims in stentorian tones the fact that he has in his show a petrified woman, recently unearthed in Arizona, and to prove the truth of this assertion, invites doctors and scientists to visit the attraction free. Proceeding north, the "educated horse" is the next show that strives to amuse the public. The promoters promise a number of things from this animal, calling him 'Independence', the horse with the human brain. After passing several cigar and confectionery stands the visitor comes to the Spanish theatre, a place where Oriental dances, a burlesque show and singing and dancing performances are given. The rest of the road is comprised principally of cigar stands, nigger baby and African dodger shows. Down on the east side of the Road a knife rack, the Egyptian queen, a palmist, and more nigger baby stands hold forth. The sacred crocodile of the Ganges, 200 years ago as the 'spieler' says, comes next in the line of amusements. Another dancing girl show, this one with genuine Dutch comedians, can be seen on the same street. Candy booths galore come next, and rounding the corner and turning up the south Road, the visitor is bewildered by the cries of the dozens of 'barkers'. On this street the athletic arena, the maze mystery, two dancing girl shows, and the merry–go–round are the principal attractions. **"**

Vancouver *Daily News–Advertiser*, 16 August 1910.

Hastings Park Grandstand, 1910

The grandstand was one of the first structures erected at Hastings Park by the Vancouver Exhibition Association. Designed primarily for crowds drawn to horse racing events, the facility also served as the site for such attractions as auto races, athletic events, band performances, and the annual opening ceremonies. The V.E.A. administration offices were housed under the stands.

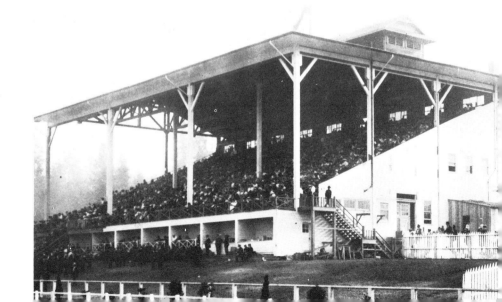

Manufacturers' Building, 1919

Spurred on by the success of the early fairs, the V.E.A. moved quickly to expand the display facilities. The building pictured here was designed to house a variety of automotive products and other industrial displays. The grounds of Hastings Park itself were maintained year round as an east end park with the well cropped lawns and forested areas serving as a welcome attraction for area residents.

Forestry Building, 1919

As part of its grand plan for the exhibition, the V.E.A. decided to feature all aspects of the British Columbian economy. A major component of that programme was the imposing Forestry Building, constructed entirely of local wood products and housing both forestry and mining exhibits. Built in 1913, the building remained in use until the 1930's when it succumbed to dry rot and had to be torn down.

Renfrew Street Near The Exhibition, 1920

From the beginning, the exhibition and traffic congestion seem to have gone hand in hand. Cars were double–parked on the shoulder of Renfrew Street as their owners rushed off to the fair. Structures in the background (left to right) include the Industrial Building, Manufacturers' Building and the Forestry Building.

Vancouver Exhibition Carnival, 1914

The midway has been one of the most consistently popular segments of the fair. As this early photo shows, the basic nature of its features have not changed very much, with a ferris wheel, contests, novelty attractions, and special "shows" all in evidence. A permanent, year–round amusement park did not appear until the early 1920's.

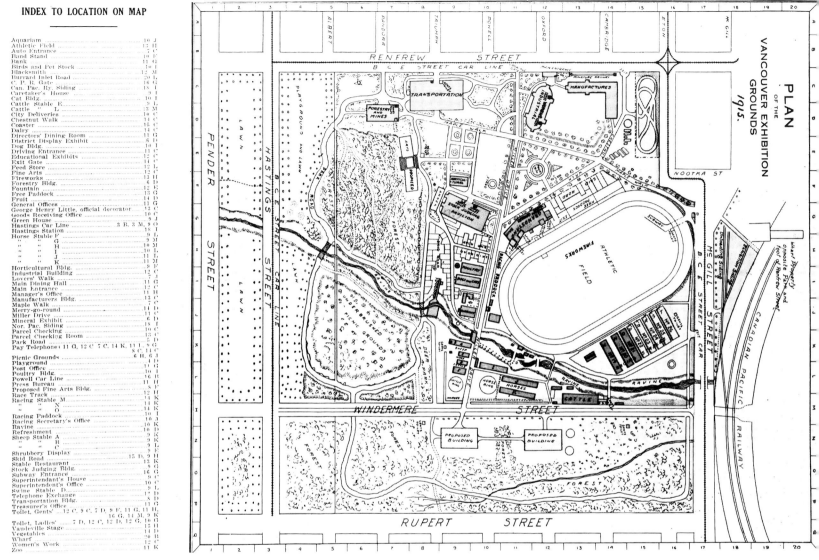

Vancouver Exhibition Grounds, 1915

By 1915, the exhibition had grown from its limited origins into a sizeable and permanent establishment. This plan shows the locations of the various exhibit and amusement facilities and also indicates the still limited development of the remainder of Hastings Park. Within ten years, most of the forested area was gone, the trees having been cut down to make way for a public golf course.

Livestock Competitions, 1917

Agriculture has played an important, if not always prominent, role in the exhibition. Subsidized by the railway companies and the Vancouver Exhibition Association, the cattle departments regularly drew large numbers of competitors, although not yet as many as the provincial exhibition at New Westminster, which, until its demise in 1930, was clearly British Columbia's premier agricultural fair.

Entrant in Livestock Competition, 1917

World War I and reduced government grants for prizes combined to severely restrict the number of entries in the various livestock competitions. As V.E.A. President Miller noted, "scarcity of help to attend cattle was the principal reason for the non–entry of many herds."
V.E.A. Bulletin, No. 8 (1917).

Service Concessions And Public Education At The Early Fairs

Many concessions, such as the Church of England Tea Tent, 1917 (left) were managed by religious or service organizations. The operations advertised the activities of the club or church and helped raise money for their various ventures. The Vancouver General Hospital Tent, 1914 (below left) was one indication of the public health concerns of social reformers in the first decades of the 20th Century. To encourage better standards of personal hygiene and medical care, members of the VGH staff used their site at the fair to answer questions and provide basic assistance with medical problems. An even more important programme was the Better Babies Contest. For a small fee, mothers could have their children assessed by medical professionals. Particularly healthy babies were awarded prizes; sick ones were sent to the hospital. Such displays and contests were credited with considerably increasing public interest in health care.

The Fair as School and Playground

❝The spirit of democracy pervades it, for under the auspices, every man, woman and child in the community can find some individual interest, no matter whether it be agricultural, industrial, commercial, educational, inventive or sublime.

Then let the people realize that at Hastings Park at their doorstep is slowly but steadily being accomplished and developed a people's gigantic public school and playground worthy of a progressive people, a progressive province and a progressive country.❞

J. J. Miller in V.E.A. *Bulletin* No. 3 (1912), p. 15.

Begg Motors Co. Display, c. 1919

One of the major industrial displays in the early years was the auto show. Immodestly referred to as the "second best" in North America, deferring only to a presentation in New York City, the show was made up of a variety of corporate exhibits similar to that of the Begg Motor Co.

Auto Racing On Hastings Park Racetrack, 1919

Always eager to add new attractions that would appeal to a wider audience, the V.E.A. continually expanded and revised the entertainment package. The auto races held on the exhibition race track were a major feature from the 'teens to the 1930's.

World War I and the Exhibition

❝Five times since the outbreak of war we have carried out an exhibition. A false idea at one time took possession of many minds that exhibitions should be closed during war time. This view was not taken by the Imperial and Dominion governments, who saw in them an influential means of educating and inspiring the people to devote their best energies to greater and better production, besides being an important factor in maintaining the commercial and social equilibrium of communities in times of danger and unrest.❞

V.E.A. *Bulletin* No. 9 (1918).

World War I Exhibition Poster
War broke out just as the 1914 exhibition was to begin. In face of considerable public debate on the propriety of holding a fair while hostilities raged, the Vancouver Exhibition Association decided to press ahead with a serious and determined theme that they felt was consistent with the new wartime environment.

VANCOUVER AUG. EXHIBITION 13-21 AGRICULTURAL AND INDUSTRIAL

BUSINESS AS USUAL

1915 VANCOUVER · EXHIBITION · ASSOCIATION BY LAND AND SEA WE PROSPER

ENTRIES CLOSE AUG. 2ND

$50,000 IN PRIZES.

REDUCED RATES ON ALL STEAMSHIP AND RAILWAY LINES

J.J.MILLER, PRES.   G.F.BALDWIN, HON-TREAS.   H.S.ROLSTON, MANAGER.

Military Procession, c. 1917

As a site for parades and patriotic gatherings, Hastings Park was unequalled in Vancouver. The racetrack and grandstand provided a fine venue for such events, and both were pressed into service on a number of occasions during World War I as Vancouverites gathered to demonstrate their commitment to the war effort.

Battalion Tents At Hastings Park, 1918

With acres of cleared ground and with a number of structures readily adaptable for military use, the Hastings Park exhibition grounds were a natural site for wartime mobilization. Numerous soldiers camped on the site prior to embarkation to join the Canadian Expeditionary Force overseas.

Drill Exercises At Hastings Park, 1918

Various pieces of military hardware and several reserve drill corps remained on the site during the fair both as an attraction and as evidence of the V.E.A.'s contribution to the war effort during World War I.

Panorama Of Hastings Park, 1919
The decision to stage an exhibition in Hastings Park was a boon to east end realtors. The opening of the fair led to the construction of a street car line to the park and encouraged development in what had been to that point a sparsely populated area of the city. As this photo shows, ten years after exhibition facilities were erected, the east side was gradually being settled.

24

2
Decade of Debate and Decision, 1920–1929

By 1920 the glow of earlier years had begun to fade. Over the next decade, attendance at the fair and the prize money offered continued to increase, but some Vancouverites began to question the role and function of the Vancouver Exhibition Association. On a number of occasions during the decade, the future of the Hastings Park exhibition was seriously in doubt.

Arguments over the association's lease of Hastings Park and discussion of a proposed amalgamation with the New Westminster exhibition diverted attention from the V.E.A.'s fair time activities. In 1925 the affairs of the exhibition were subjected to a full –scale civic investigation, and the controversy about who should exercise control over the exhibition ended only when the directors of the association threatened to resign en masse if they were not given a free hand to manage the fair.

Though the debate ended with the decision that the Vancouver Exhibition Association would continue; its role was clearly changing. It was becoming more difficult to hold on to such an important piece of real estate as Hastings Park to use it only for a week long fair. Accepting the challenge, the V.E.A. moved to accommodate the public's demand for both a fair and a recreational centre. They tried harder to provide a variety of activities and attractions on the grounds on a year round basis. Exhibition buildings were made available for conventions and meetings, a small zoo was opened, Vancouver's first public golf course was built and operated, an aquarium was provided, and the V.E.A. even erected and maintained a major campground.

Entrance To The Grounds, 1929

From 1910 to 1920, the main entrance to the grounds was located on the northwest corner near Powell Street. City Council's decision to widen and pave Hastings Street in 1920 encouraged the V.E.A. to re–orient the grounds around the southwest entrance, shown in the above photo.

Shoot–The–Chutes, 1920's

The permanent midway, an integral part of Hastings Park from the early 1920's, was a favourite Vancouver recreational centre, providing employment for east end youths and amusement for people from all parts of the lower mainland.

One of the most prominent attractions of the early midway was the Shoot-the-Chutes. People waited in long lines for the chance to enjoy a quick descent down the water ramp in the heavy wooden boats. The other major rides were two roller coasters, the Giant and Baby Dippers, the former being so terrifying that local myth suggests that it was a fairly reliable abortificant.

27

Concessionaries Row, 1930

The concession area has always been a major attraction at the exhibition. In the background is the entrance to the major rides. Other features of this area included bingo, slot machines, gambling wheels, shooting galleries, novelty stands, and food concessions.

28

An Outside View of Vancouver's Fair

"When in British Columbia I learned that while the Westminster people were willing to join with Vancouver in establishing a fair on neutral ground, Vancouver on the other hand, was quite willing to join but only providing Westminster closed their gates and went over to Hastings Park.

Westminster, as you and I well know, runs a good Agricultural Fair and does not pay freight charges to get live stock exhibits. Vancouver never has been a real agricultural fair and has resorted to very questionable means to get exhibits.**"**

C. M. McRae, Acting Live Stock Commissioner to Dr. J. H. Grisdale, Deputy Minister of Agriculture, Ottawa, 21 December 1928.

Dog Show, 1928
Such events as the annual Dog Show, Cat Show, Cage Bird, and Rabbit Show, were prominent features of the fair. Often representing the highest level of competition in the province, these shows typically attracted entries from throughout the Pacific Northwest.

Big City Aspirations

"The oft repeated aspiration of being the "Toronto of the West" is now being realized.**"**

Vancouver Exhibition Association *Bulletin* No. 16 (1925), p. 11.

Pageants In Outdoor Theatre, 1927
As part of its entertainment package, the V.E.A. offered free attractions. Roving bands, vaudeville acts and daredevil displays vied with the midway and the exhibits for the fairgoers' attention. Pageants, usually presented by amateur groups, were a regular feature and included shows such as this one on human values and a re–enactment of the construction of the Canadian Pacific Railway.

Beauties And A Beast, 1927

The fair always incorporated a variety of elements into the entertainment part of its programme. These young ladies represented the height of swimsuit fashion and feminine beauty in the 1920's.

City Home/Country Home, 1922

The V.E.A. saw the fair as an important meeting place between city and country. Displays such as this one which catered to both groups and illustrated the different needs and lifestyles of city and country were familiar features.

Jo–To Medicine Display, 1922

Many entrepreneurs in Vancouver seized on the exhibition as an excellent means of bringing their new products to the attention of thousands of local residents. Jo–To Medicine, which was offered for sale at the exhibit, promised relief from a variety of stomach and internal maladies, and is a good example of such a commercial display.

Fraser Valley Milk Producers Association, 1926

At the fair agriculturalists also offered their products to a large urban audience. This particular association was among the many regular exhibitors at the fair.

Vancouver Versus New Westminster: Agricultural Fair or Industrial Exhibition

66In fact, the whole Vancouver Exhibition has gone ahead rapidly far more as an industrial than an agricultural show . . . Is it not too bad that some Federal influence cannot induce Vancouver and New Westminster Shows to get together and put on one really good show with facilities for a winter fair, rather than have these two competing expensive exhibitions so close to each other, one developing more along industrial lines and the other with healthy deficits attempting to feature agriculture?**99**

E. S. Archibald, Director, Experimental Farms to Deputy Minister, Federal Department of Agriculture, 4 April 1929.

Jarvis Electric Co. Displays, 1924 and 1926

The marketing function of the exhibition display was well understood, and the fact that most exhibitors returned year after year suggests that their efforts proved profitable. The Jarvis Electric Co. used its booth to display and sell its alternative to the "outdated" ice–box, and highlight the new variety of appliances on the market.

Ford Equipment Display, 1926

Farmers, contractors and the general public interested in recent developments in a variety of industries often got a first glimpse of technological change at the fair. Companies such as the Ford Motor Co. exhibited their most recent and innovative products to large numbers of prospective customers.

Columbia Aviation Display, 1924

It was clear in the 1920's that aviation was the transportation technology of the future. In earlier fairs the aeroplane had only appeared as a special feature or attraction. By the mid–1920's, aviation displays appeared with greater frequency, with this firm advertising not only its operation, but also flying lessons.

Boosterism and the Fair

❝The Vancouver Exhibition . . . possesses a unique opportunity of becoming the great show room, the sample house, the great publicity bureau, the great educator and exponent of the wonderful God–given resources of the country.**❞**

V.E.A. *Bulletin* No. 11 (1920), p. 16.

Politics And The Fair

An established and well-attended urban exhibition could always exert a little political clout if the occasion warranted.

❝To Hon. W. R. Motherwell, Federal Minister of Agriculture Nov. 1, 1926

Doctor King has handed us your wire declining request for relief [from] tuberculin regulations for market beef cattle [at] Winter Fair [in] Vancouver. In belief you will yet grant application when full particulars are before you we are making [a] final appeal for consideration.

E. S. Knowlton, President, Vancouver Centre Liberal Assoc.; David McKenzie, Pres., Burrard Liberal Assoc.; W. McDonald, Pres., Vancouver South Liberal Assoc.; A. McGougan, Pres., North Vancouver Liberal Assoc.; R. McLennan, Ex-Liberal Candidate and Pres., Vancouver Exhibition Association; W. C. Brown, Past Pres., Liberal Assoc. and Director Exhibition Association; A. D. Patterson, Liberal M.L.A. and Director Exhibition Association**❞**

"Buy B.C." Display, 1927

Vancouver's exhibition remained loyal to its one main purpose — to encourage the growth and development of local and regional industry. The boosterism of the V.E.A.'s presentation is clearly evident in this booth encouraging fairgoers to favour local producers with their business.

Kraft Foods Display Booth, 1928

Summerland Experimental Station Exhibit, 1922

The federal government was actively involved with major fairs, funding construction projects, setting and enforcing regulations for livestock competitions and hosting displays reflecting their role in experimental agriculture. The experimental stations used their exhibit at the fair to draw attention to their activities and more importantly to chart progress in agricultural technology and production.

66 The whole object of our wishing to have the Indians here is to show the development which is taking place under the administration of the department [of Indian Affairs] and . . . to have a large display from various Indian reservations and schools of basketry work, vegetables and other evidences of the industry of the Indians. **99**

J. K. Matheson to Dr. Duncan Scott, 13 December 1927

Kamloops Indian School Display, 1924

The V.E.A. had always set aside space for local and provincial schools to exhibit handicrafts and school projects. Institutions involved in these productions included secondary and night schools, vocational institutes and, as shown here, Indian residential schools. These latter displays were designed to show that under the close guidance of their teachers, native children were learning the requisite skills to advance themselves.

Postal Education Exhibit, 1923

Eager to explain their programmes and services to as large an audience as possible, various government departments hosted displays at the fair. In this instance, the Post Office was attempting to educate the public on the uses and purposes of the postal system.

Gas Station At Hastings Park Auto Camp, 1924

As a condition of its 1923 lease for Hastings Park, the V.E.A. was required to build and maintain an auto camp. The gas station doubled as the office.

Campers At Hastings Park, 1924

The Hastings Park Auto Camp was one of the first such facilities in the Vancouver area, and during its brief existence, it served as a popular resting spot for visitors. Camping as a regular recreational activity was still in an embryonic stage and had not yet expanded into a mass participation activity. For a short time, however, the camp attracted a steady stream of campers, many from the United States.

Self Defence: Reply To The Critics Of The Fair

"Every citizen is or ought to be interested in fine arts, horticulture, women's work, horse show, cattle, sheep and swine exhibits, poultry, cage birds, pet stock, dogs, cats, minerals, school exhibits, industries and manufacturers and many other departments of the Exhibition. In fact, in many of these departments the greater number of exhibits come from the citizens. The citizen has his hobbies, his interests, his business. In these features he is pleased to learn what the other fellow is doing. He is anxious to find out by comparison where he stands, and in any of these departments held in separate shows by themselves are never so successful or even possible as when shown collectively where the most successful ones financially can be made to carry the others which do not command sufficient patronage to justify their being held.

Advantages to the city industrial exhibitor. This can be summed up in a very few words as follows: The exhibitor would not fill up every inch of space available, pay large moneys for their space and go to a great deal of expense unless it paid them well to do so, and when we say that we cannot begin to accomodate all the applications for space that we have, and many of the exhibitors reserve their space every year and have done so from the very first, we think we say all that is necessary.**"**

V.E.A., *Replies to Resolutions and Questions Submitted by the Civic Committee to the Vancouver Exhibition Association* (excerpts), 1925.

40

East End Of Vancouver, 1929

This photo gives an excellent indication of the geographic relationship between the exhibition and the City of Vancouver. The major buildings of the downtown area are on the horizon while New Brighton Beach, in the foreground, was the site of considerable industrial activity.

3
Prosperity in Times of Trouble, 1930–1939

While Canada and Canadians reeled under the impact of the Great Depression, exhibitions and fairs ironically enjoyed heightened popularity. In Vancouver, the exhibition attracted growing numbers of spectators, rising from around 200,000 in the mid–1920's to 377,000 in 1936, and the association's financial returns mounted steadily. Exhibitions have always had a release or escapist dimension, giving people a chance to leave the drudgery of everyday life for the vitality and exuberance of the fair, and this role was never more noticeable than in the Depression years. Facing lower wages or even unemployment, Vancouverites turned to the one institution that continued to provide a truly positive outlook on the future. The fair continued to boost Vancouver, offering proof and promises that the city would soon escape from the economic doldrums and rise to its destined place in the sun. This theme was encompassed in the 1932 "Back to Prosperity Fair."

The Vancouver Exhibition Association did not get through the Depression unscathed. The bad management and consequent bankruptcy of the operators of the amusement complex at Hastings Park caused short–term distress, but the decision of the creditors to form a new amusement company enabled the carnival to continue uninterrupted. A more serious crisis hit late in 1936 when one of the association's accountants was convicted of embezzlement, having stolen $41,000 from civic relief funds administered by the exhibition association. The resulting furor led to yet another civic investigation of the V.E.A., but an internal re–organization quickly dissipated the controversy.

Despite these setbacks and the poor economic climate, the Vancouver exhibition grew substantially. Aided by provincial, federal, and civic grants for relief projects, the Vancouver Exhibition Association was able to continue its physical expansion of Hastings Park, adding in particular the Renfrew Complex (Forum, Pure Foods and Women's Buildings). As well, the final closure of the New Westminster exhibition in 1930 left Vancouver as the paramount fair in the province. In response to its new found status, the V.E.A. altered its presentation, expanding its agricultural department significantly and moving to fulfil its long–held aspirations of becoming the showcase not only of Vancouver, but of all British Columbia.

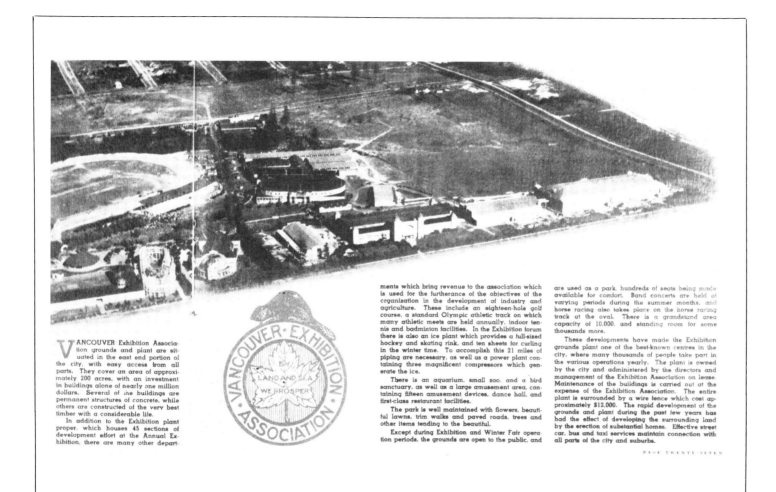

VANCOUVER Exhibition Association grounds and plant are situated in the east end portion of the city, with easy access from all parts. They cover an area of approximately 200 acres, with an investment in buildings alone of nearly one million dollars. Several of the buildings are permanent structures of concrete, while others are constructed of the very best timber with a considerable life.

In addition to the Exhibition plant proper, which houses 45 sections of development effort at the Annual Exhibition, there are many other depart-ments which bring revenue to the association which is used for the furtherance of the objectives of the organization in the development of industry and agriculture. These include an eighteen-hole golf course, a standard Olympic athletic track on which many athletic meets are held annually, indoor tennis and badminton facilities. In the Exhibition forum there is also an ice plant which provides a full-sized hockey and skating rink, and ten sheets for curling in the winter time. To accomplish this 21 miles of piping are necessary, as well as a power plant containing three magnificent compressors which generate the ice.

There is an aquarium, small zoo, and a bird sanctuary, as well as a large amusement area, containing fifteen amusement devices, dance hall, and first-class restaurant facilities.

The park is well maintained with flowers, beautiful lawns, trim walks and paved roads, trees and other items tending to the beautiful.

Except during Exhibition and Winter Fair operation periods, the grounds are open to the public, and are used as a park, hundreds of seats being made available for comfort. Band concerts are held at varying periods during the summer months, and horse racing also takes place on the horse racing track at the oval. There is a grandstand area capacity of 10,000, and standing room for some thousands more.

These developments have made the Exhibition grounds plant one of the best-known centres in the city, where many thousands of people take part in the various operations yearly. The plant is owned by the city and administered by the directors and management of the Exhibition Association on lease. Maintenance of the buildings is carried out at the expense of the Exhibition Association. The entire plant is surrounded by a wire fence which cost approximately $12,000. The rapid development of the grounds and plant during the past few years has had the effect of developing the surrounding land by the erection of substantial homes. Effective street car, bus and taxi services maintain connection with all parts of the city and suburbs.

PAGE TWENTY SEVEN

Aerial View of Hastings Park, 1936

The directors and members of the Vancouver Exhibition Association were intensely proud of their contribution to their city and region. This photo is from a souvenir booklet published by the V.E.A. in conjunction with Vancouver's Golden Anniversary celebration of 1936.

Vancouver Exhibition Association, *Fifty Years of Progress* (pp. 26-27).

Amusement area, 1930's
The view is different, but the content of the amusement area in the 1930's looks strikingly familiar. Rides, puppet shows, hot dog and hamburger stands, a rifle range, bingo and houses of mystery are all long–time carnival standards. The amusement area pictured here was located just north of the present Pacific Coliseum. Note that the Hastings Park forests so noticeable in the early years have been cut down. The golf course is in the background.

Daily Province Rest Tent and Creche, 1932

The Vancouver Daily Province *newspaper sponsored this rest tent for weary walkers and a supervised playground for young children.*

T. B. Lee Fashion Show, 1933

Winter Indoor Tennis in Horseshow Building, 1930's

Golf Course on Exhibition Grounds, 1930's

Installation of Ice in the Forum, 1930

Backed by $300,000 from a civic by–law, the V.E.A. was able to erect three large buildings, the Forum, Pure Foods and Women's Buildings, in 1930. The first structure was designed to house ice hockey and could also handle major entertainment events. When completed, the ice surface in the Forum was the largest sheet of artificial ice in North America. Designed to withstand twice Vancouver's heaviest recorded snowfall, the Forum roof collapsed on January 21, 1935 after an extended snowfall, resulting in acrimonious debate between Vancouver City Council and the V.E.A. over financial responsibility for reconstruction.

Agricultural Display, 1932
With the collapse of the New Westminster Exhibition in 1930, following a fire which destroyed the buildings at Queen's Park, Vancouver's show became the major agricultural event in the province.

Livestock Competition, 1930

The V.E.A. continued to offer a full competitive programme in the livestock section and the size of its prize lists made it the envy of every other fair in Western Canada. Seldom headlining the fair, the livestock shows and heavy horse competitions nonetheless drew an ever increasing number of entries.

Woodward's Draft Team, 1933

Junior Farmers' Competition, 1930's

For many years, the Junior Farmers' show was operated as an adjunct of the livestock competition and hence received comparatively limited attention. To many agriculturalists, including the B.C. Department of Agriculture, encouraging young men and women to pursue farming careers was of the utmost importance to the future of Canadian agriculture and the Junior Farmer programme was expanded accordingly.

Livestock, 1934

National Egg Show, 1930
The National Egg Show was a combination retail/producer presentation designed to explain the production and uses of eggs and egg by–products.

Honey Display, 1938
Various commercial producers provided samples of their honey products, which were then judged according to the quality of the product and presentation. By the 1950's, such competitive shows were gone, replaced by producer association displays on the production and uses of farm products.

Richmond Display of Produce, 1930
Regional displays of agricultural production formed an integral part of the agricultural show at the exhibition. Towns and regions throughout the province sent collections of their best local produce to the fair where they served as a useful advertisement of the agricultural potential of the area.

Opening Day Parade, 1935

The opening of the exhibition provided a ready occasion for celebration, but until 1935 the festivities were restricted to small processions of dignitaries through city streets and inaugural ceremonies on the grounds. In the midst of the Depression and at the urging of Vancouver mayor G. G. McGeer, the V.E.A. decided to stage an opening day parade featuring bands, drill teams, clowns, business and service clubs, and community floats. The parade was a major success and was integrated into the annual exhibition programme.

B. C. Electric Company Float, 1935

52

Vancouver Publicity Bureau Float, 1935

Iron Fireman Automatic Coal Burner Float, 1935

54

B. C. Telephone Company Float, 1935

Scottish Dancers, 1934

As part of their programme of free attractions, the V.E.A. relied heavily on amateur productions. Groups like these Scottish Dancers were only too willing to take advantage of the opportunity to perform before a fair–time audience. For many young entertainers, the chance to dance, sing, act or show one's acrobatic prowess at the exhibition was the high-light of a budding career.

Gold Panning Demonstration, 1934

Informational demonstrations such as this one for gold pan-ning were both educational and entertaining, and helped draw crowds to the fair.

Midland Coal Co. Display, and B.C. Electric Gas Division, 1932

The commercial exhibitors at the fair often engaged in vigorous competiion. In the 1930's, the main battle was between various energy concerns. Coal distributors fought to retain their markets in the face of mounting competition from rival firms extolling the virtues of manufactured gas or electricity.

B.C. Electric Farm Power Exhibit, 1934

If the fair served as an important market place for city dwellers, it was of even greater value to companies interested in reaching a rural market. The exhibition offered a rare opportunity to contact large numbers of farmers in a short period of time. As a result, companies such as B.C. Electric annually hosted major displays of wares and services of potential interest to the farming community.

Vancouver Fire Department Exhibit, 1937

The exhibition has always served as an important forum for government departments or agencies who wanted to spread information to the public. This display by the Vancouver Fire Department was a particularly effective means of encouraging fire prevention.

Greater Vancouver Health League Display, 1937

As a means of reaching large numbers of prospective clients and describing an organization's services, an exhibit at the fair had few equals. The Greater Vancouver Health League used its booth to hand out materials on their activities and to encourage interest in, and knowledge of, hygiene, disease, posture, and nutrition.

Mining Exhibit, 1937

The V.E.A. was always particularly interested in encouraging the development of the province's natural resources. Forestry exhibits, a fisheries display, and this presentation on B.C. mining were designed to inform the fairgoers of the great bounty to be found in British Columbia. The mining display incorporated examples of ore as well as diagrams and models of mines in operation.

Exhibition Prize Home, 1934
As a special attraction in 1934, a two–storey home constructed and furnished exclusively with products from British Columbia was erected at Hastings Park. For the duration of the exhibition, the home was open to fairgoers, serving as a useful display of local materials and manufacturers. Tickets were sold and at the end of the fair, the home was raffled off. The idea of a prize home had first been used in the 1920's, but the dwellings offered in that decade were much less impressive than the 1934 home. Most often, the main exhibition draw featured automobiles, trips around the world, or cash as prizes.

4

Vancouver's Exhibition in Wartime, 1939–1946

When the pall of war replaced the gloom of the depression, the Vancouver Exhibition Association was required to alter its presentation once again. In 1940 and 1941, the military dominated both the parade and the annual fair. Displays of army hardware, soldiers' drill corps, and floats designed around patriotic themes highlighted the parade, while recruiting booths, war savings certificate displays, and exhibits extolling the virtues of assisting the war effort filled the grounds. It was "All Out for Victory", and the exhibition was prepared to do its part to aid the national war effort.

Like many other exhibitions across the country, the Vancouver fair was unable to keep operating throughout the war years. The facilities erected for the fair were useful for military purposes, and as the need for such buildings increased so too did the pressure on the Vancouver Exhibition Association to vacate the grounds. When Pearl Harbor was attacked in December of 1941, the matter assumed a new urgency. For a variety of reasons, few of them military, the federal government decided to "evacuate" all persons of Japanese descent, most of whom were Canadians, from the British Columbia coast and relocate them in interior camps. Hastings Park served as the "processing centre", and in the summer of 1942 over eight thousand Japanese–Canadians passed through the grounds on their way inland. With the evacuation completed, the federal government retained its control of the grounds, using the facilities for storage, as a manning centre for the armed forces, and as a drill practice area, thus compelling the cancellation of fair activities at Hastings Park from 1942 to 1946.

The Vancouver Exhibition Association nonetheless continued to offer some activities elsewhere. Most important, the association kept itself occupied with planning and preparation for future fairs, acquiring land for expansion, conducting a thorough investigation of the grounds and projecting further development. The association took advantage of the hiatus to ensure that when the war finally ended, British Columbians would be greeted by a fair that was bigger, more modern, and more convenient than ever. As if to signal the coming of a "new look" exhibition, a brand new name was selected in 1946. Hereafter, Vancouver's fair was to be the Pacific National Exhibition.

"Britannia Rules the Waves" Float, 1941

Military Drill Corps on Parade, 1941

Parade, 1941

Military themes not surprisingly dominated both the 1940 and 1941 exhibitions. The parade had a particularly military flair, with marching bands, drill corps, and armed forces hardware serving as the focus for the attraction. Many of the floats, such as the one shown here, were designed around war themes, encouraging Vancouverites to assist the war effort to the fullest.

Encouraging the War Effort, 1941

Inside the exhibition, just as in the parade, the war was the theme for a number of booths and displays. The government staged a series of exhibits designed to encourage the purchase of war savings certificates while also offering other attractions which informed citizens of ways in which they could help the war effort.

Royal Canadian Air Force Display, 1941

In 1940 and 1941, the various branches of the Canadian armed forces put considerable effort into explaining their activities and attempting to secure recruits. Through a display of their men in action, the Royal Canadian Air Force hoped to convince young men to join the air arm.

Crowds and Midway, 1940

A fair is never a static entity. Instead, it changes with the community in which it is located and with the values and aspirations of the people who patronize the show. As a result, Vancouver's fair has undergone some major changes in its seven decades. This 1940 photo shows a "Nudist Village" and a variety of other risqué exhibits. Such attractions were not in evidence at the first fair nor can they be found at the fair now (although their demise is fairly recent). The appearance of such features provides a useful insight into the changing entertainment demands of Vancouverites.

Agricultural Fair or Industrial Exhibition

"While agriculture in all its phases has been, and will continue to be, of major importance, it has for some time past been the opinion of the Board of Control that insufficient attention has been given to other phases of our provincial industrial activities and that henceforth lumbering, mining, fishing, manufacturing, merchandising and tourist travel must be vigorously and aggressively sponsored and featured.**"**

V.E.A. *Bulletin* No. 34 (1943).

Dancers, Outdoor Stage, 1940

Outdoor Stage, 1940
Free entertainment was always an important feature of the fair. As the exhibition became more sophisticated, it became necessary to offer more elaborate facilities for the entertainers. The outdoor stage was the site of the opening ceremonies and a variety of other features, ranging from professional singers to amateur acrobats and dance troupes.

Children's Aeroplane Ride, 1940

Although the basic concept behind the various rides has remained fairly standard, the theme behind the attractions has changed with the times. In the 1940's, an aeroplane provided a delightful thrill for children, much like spaceships and moon walks would do in later years.

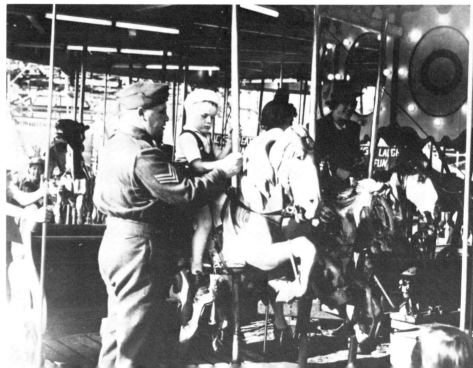

Children's Ride, 1940

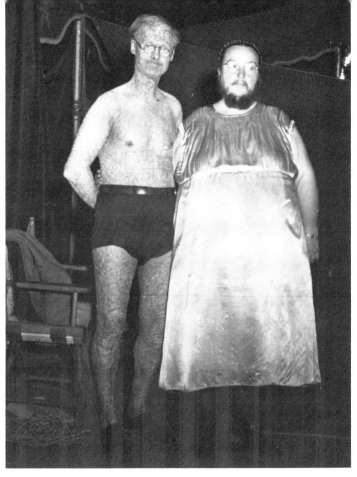

Fat Lady and Man with Alligator Skin at the Freak Show, 1941

"Freak Show", 1941

From 1910, the infamous "freak shows" were a regular feature along the midway. In the first year of the fair, there were such dubious attractions as a petrified woman and a "horse with a human brain". This show included a four-legged woman, a fat lady, midgets and a man with "alligator" skin.

Midgets at the "Freak Show", 1941

B.C. Telephone Co. "How to Use the Dial Telephone", 1940

Utility companies frequently used their displays to explain technological advances. When B.C. Telephone introduced the dial telephone and long distance phone calls, they set up a major exhibit to introduce these remarkable innovations.

Pure Foods "Sample House", 1939

One of the principal commercial functions of the fair was to serve as a "sample house", a place where consumers could try out all that was new and innovative in the marketplace. The Pure Foods Building was a favourite of fairgoers as exhibitors freely dispensed samples of their food products.

Cars parked on Hastings Park Golf Course, 1941

The golf course served a number of functions for the V.E.A., not the least of which was as a readily available parking lot. A more important function of the course was to provide land for the expansion of the exhibition. Whenever more area was needed it was simply carved off the golf course and additional land for the course was tagged on elsewhere.

Lipsett Indian Museum, 1941

The Lipsett Indian Museum was a major addition to the V.E.A.'s operations. Donated in 1941 by Edward and Mary Lipsett, members of the association, the museum included an excellent collection of American Indian artifacts. The new attraction displaced the aquarium, which had been a fixture in the building for almost two decades. The museum was later moved to the B.C. Building where it remained until it was transferred to Vancouver's new Centennial Museum in 1971.

War-time Use of PNE Facilities

"We go on record as being wholeheartedly behind the Department (of Defence) in their war effort and as not wanting to do anything that will interfere with that but just as soon as the Department decides that they have no further use for the buildings, we shall be glad to have them returned to us . . .**"**

Minutes of the Executive Committee, V.E.A., 15 November 1944.

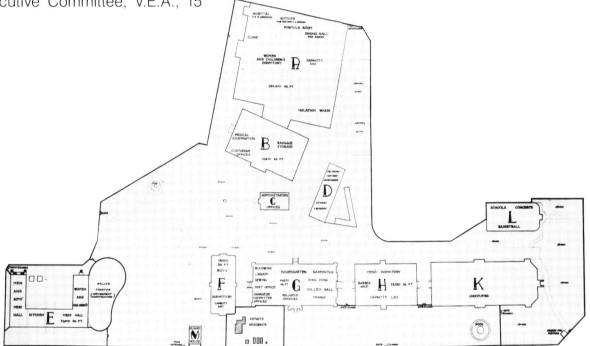

Hastings Park as Evacuation Centre, 1942

When the Federal government succumbed to public pressure in 1942 and decided to evacuate the Japanese–Canadians from the B.C. coast, Hastings Park was pressed into service and a fence was hastily erected around a section of the grounds. Women and young children were separated from the men and older boys. A variety of services were set up, including schools, a hospital, a small store, and recreational facilities.

71

Japanese Women's Dormitory, 1942

"The whole place is impregnated with the smell of ancient manure and maggots. Every other day it is swept with dichlorine of lime, or something, but you can't disguise horse smell, cow smell, sheep, pigs, rabbits and goats. And it is dusty! The toilets are just a sheet metal trough, and up until now they did not have partitions or seats. The women kicked so they put up partitions and a terribly makeshift seat. Twelve–year–old boys stay with the women too, you know . . . as for the bunks, they were the most tragic things there. Steel and wooden frames with a thin lumpy straw tick, a bolster, and three army blankets . . . no sheets unless you bring your own. These are the "homes" of the women I saw . . . these bunks were hung with sheets and blankets and clothes of every hue and variety — a regular gypsy tent of colours, age and cleanliness — all hung in a pathetic attempt at privacy . . . an old, old lady was crying, saying she would rather have died than have to come to such a place . . . there are ten showers for 1,500 women.**"**

Muriel Fujiwara Kitagawa to Wesley Kitagawa, 20 April 1942.

Japanese Men's Dormitory, 1942

The living conditions were far from comfortable, as thousands were crammed into barely adequate facilities. This massive collection of bunk beds was the dormitory for all the men and older boys. More than eight thousand persons of Japanese descent passed through the camp between March and September, 1942. For most, the days in Hastings Park were fairly short, since the camp was intended primarily as a way station for people destined for resettlement in the interior of the province.

Meal Time, Men's Mess and Laundry Room, 1942

For the Japanese Canadians housed on the grounds, the regular routine of life had to go on. In providing these basic needs, efficiency was the by–word. Later, the British Columbia Security Commission was able to report with undisguised pride that it had managed to provide 1,542,371 meals at a "raw food cost" of 9.33¢ per meal.

Boys and Girls Department, Chilliwack, 1945

When the exhibition was shut down between 1942 and 1946, the V.E.A. was determined that one very important part of their programme not suffer. The Boys and Girls Department continued its operations throughout the war, although all events were staged in Chilliwack in conjunction with that city's exhibition.

5
Expansion and New Directions, 1947–1960

With the war over and the fair renamed the Pacific National Exhibition, it emerged with a new look in 1947. In this fair and over the next decade, it was clear that a different exhibition had emerged from the war years, one that was more "professional" and business–like in its approach. Without a fair for five years, Vancouverites swarmed enthusiastically to the first post–war fair, pushing week long attendance to close to 600,000. Particular importance was placed on the appearance of "big–name" American personalities, with acts such as Jimmy Durante and Edgar Bergen headlining the fair.

The new professionalism was soon evident in other areas as well, as the P.N.E. expanded its offerings ever more widely. The Miss PNE contest was held for the first time in 1948, the Shrine Circus was added as an annual attraction, and special features such as a giant ski–jump increased interest in the fair. The exhibition was clearly changing, with the traditional focus on industrial displays and agricultural competitions fading to the background somewhat to be replaced by entertainment extravaganzas. The 1950's were heady years for the association, as Vancouverites and British Columbians flocked in ever larger numbers to the fair and backed P.N.E. plans further by supporting the construction of such facilities as the B.C. Building and Empire Stadium.

Just as the fair was changing, so too was the range of activities at the newly named Exhibition Park. The P.N.E. was pushing aggressively into a variety of areas with the Western Hockey League Vancouver Canucks playing out of the Forum and the B.C. Lions, new additions to the Canadian Football League, occupying Empire Stadium. The latter facility, serving as the focus for much that was new at the P.N.E. had come to Exhibition Park following the City of Vancouver's successful bid to host the 1954 British Empire Games.

Responding to Vancouver's growing maturity and enhanced aspirations, the P.N.E. was forced to change and was expected to search out the new, the famous and the prestigious. The Pacific National Exhibition was largely successful in its efforts to put Vancouver in league with other big cities on the continent by offering top–flight entertainment and professional sports and greatly expanding non–fair activities to meet the many and varied demands being placed on the exhibition association.

Children Watching the Parade, 1950's

P.N.E. Parade, 1947
After a five–year hiatus, the reappearance of the parade in 1947 drew thousands to the streets of Vancouver. The tightly organized spectacle of bands, drill teams, commercial and regional floats, and the ever present clowns, was an appropriate re–opening to the annual fair.

Esso Steel Band Float, 1950's

Cement Trucks on Parade, 1950's

The Aftermath — Litter, 1950's

Aerial View of the Grounds, 1949
Few physical changes are noticeable in this photo. The golf course is still in evidence, and Happyland is still located to the north of the present Pacific Coliseum. In the background, however, several blocks of homes are in the process of being cleared. That land had been purchased by the P.N.E. to allow for the expansion of the golf course.

The Gates, Outside, 1955

The Gates, Inside, 1955

Shrine—Polack Brothers Circus, 1950's

For many years, the circus had competed with the P.N.E., and on several occasions the Exhibition Association had even solicited the assistance of Vancouver City Council in order to prevent a clash of dates between the two events. An agreeable compromise was reached in the early 1950's when the P.N.E. decided to feature the Shrine—Polack Bros. Circus. For the next decade, the Circus regularly filled the Forum by offering an array of exotic, death—defying and humorous attractions.

B.C. Electric Garden Rendezvous, 1949

Just as the Vancouver Daily Province *had done in years past, the B.C. Electric Company offered weary fairgoers a place to rest amidst the whirl of the exhibition. The attractive rest area included canopied tables, chairs, and even a model hydro electric plant.*

First Old–Timers Hockey Game at the Forum, 1947

The first Old–Timers game staged in Canada was held at the PNE Forum. Among the players was Fred Taylor (back row, third from right). Dubbed "Cyclone" because of his amazing speed, Taylor was one of hockey's all time greats. He joined the Vancouver Millionaires in 1911 and led the club to Vancouver's only Stanley Cup win in 1915. Named Vancouver's citizen of the year in 1966, Taylor died June 9, 1979, at 94.

Vancouver Canucks in the Forum, 1950's

P.N.E. Happyland, 1949
Although the Big Dipper had been demolished for safety reasons, most of the presentations had changed little. The concessionaires' area was designed in an interesting circular fashion. Persons entering the grounds found their way in very easily; getting out was a more formidable task.

Guess Your Age Booth, 1955

Aerial Act, 1950's

"Fairplay on the Midway", 1950's

Man with Snakes, 1950's

Kiddieland Crowd, 1950's

Jimmy Durante Headlines the P.N.E., 1948

The most visible sign of the new "professionalism" of the post-war fair was the hiring of "big-time" American performers, like Jimmy Durante, to offer stage shows inside the Forum. The public was not as receptive as expected, and several years later the P.N.E. decided to present the Shrine Circus in that facility instead.

Demolition of the Shoot–the–Chutes, 1957

In 1957 the P.N.E. decided that Happyland had to come down. The amusement centre was relocated along Hastings Street between Empire Stadium and the B.C. Building. The intention was to modernize the facility, and the result was the destruction of several Vancouver landmarks. The Shoot–the–Chutes ride, a long-time favourite, was torn down as part of the renovation.

World of Fashion, 1948

This fashion show, held in 1948, was not a new addition. Such presentations had long been a regular feature of the fair. The ladies' dress gives an interesting perspective on the "best" in women's fashion at this particular time.

Miss PNE Contestants, 1954

Attempting to find new attractions for its post–war fair, always conscious of American examples and ever eager to involve towns and cities around the province in the exhibition, the P.N.E. decided to host a Miss PNE pageant in 1948. Various centres were given franchises in the competition, allowing them to hold local competitions to select their contestant. The winner became the P.N.E.'s representative for a year, accompanying the P.N.E. float to a variety of Pacific Northwest fairs and reigning as Queen of the Pacific National Exhibition.

Giant Ski–Jump, 1958

In conjunction with the 1958 B.C. Centennial, the P.N.E. staged a variety of special features at the fair. The most notable was the ski–jumping competition held in Empire Stadium. Thousands watched the event, though most chose to view the show from outside the stadium rather than pay for a seat inside, which meant that financially the event was something of a disaster.

Project "X", 1958

As part of the Centennial year exhibition, the P.N.E. planned a "secret" Project "X", which was kept under wraps until the eve of the fair. Project X turned out to be a display of modern rocketry and included exhibits by the American Army and the Canadian Legion. The attraction is indicative of the P.N.E.'s eagerness to identify with important provincial celebrations.

Prize Home, c. 1957

The idea of presenting a display home on the P.N.E. grounds was first adopted in the 1920's when homes were raffled off as part of the exhibition prize show. For much of the 1950's, the prize home was a small Pan–Abode, but as time passed a more substantial dwelling was offered and became a high-profile feature of the fair.

B.C. Department of Education, 1953

Government departments have been prominent exhibitors at the P.N.E. from the inception of the fair. The displays in the 1950's and later were more elaborate, but the purpose remained the same — to tell the fairgoers what the government was doing on their behalf and to instruct them on how to take advantage of public services.

Hobby Show Crowds, 1949
Toothpick Carnival, 1950

Model Train, 1951

Hobby Show, 1950's

From the first fair, when displays of "women's work" and school children's work were prominently featured, handicrafts have been an integral part of the fair. In the 1950's, the hobby show was a major attraction, drawing large crowds to view a remarkable array of the best the province's crafts people had to offer.

B.C. Tree Fruits Ltd. Display, 1953

The agricultural show of the 1950's was different than its 1930's counterpart. Beginning with the dairy industry, the agricultural exhibitors began to abandon competitive events which had been designed to promote excellence in favour of educational features, such as this B.C. Tree Fruits display, a corporate presentation designed to inform consumers of the uses and value of the products of the provincial orchard industry.

Sample Booth, Pure Foods Building, 1950's

Horticultural Show, 1949
With the advent of the more entertainment oriented fairs after World War II, agriculture assumed a less prominent place in the exhibition. When the Forum was taken over by the circus, the still large horticultural component was displaced, and as building after building was taken over for other uses, the agricultural/horticultural presentations became progressively smaller.

The PNE, An Agricultural Fair

"We are an agricultural fair and will always remain so. We are a member of the great family of fairs throughout this Province, across the dominion and across the border.**"**

Minutes of Annual General Meeting, P.N.E. December 12, 1957.

4–H and Future Farmers of Canada Show, 1950's
The junior farmers' competitions, organized by the 4–H and F.F.C. clubs, were an important agricultural attraction. As a special feature in this decade, the P.N.E. also arranged to have two 4–H members from such places as Japan, Israel and Peru visit the fair and participate in the 4–H show.

Soccer at Callister Exhibition Park, c. 1950

Before the construction of Empire Stadium in 1954, Callister Exhibition Park was the most important outdoor sports facility in Vancouver. Large crowds were drawn to the park to watch Pacific Coast League soccer games and international exhibition matches. Once Empire Stadium was built, Callister Park fell into relative disuse and began to deteriorate. The P.N.E. continued to operate the facility until 1969 when it was turned over to the city in exchange for the cost of providing artificial turf for Empire Stadium. During the exhibition, Callister Park was pressed into service as a much needed parking lot.

94

British Empire Games Opening Ceremonies, 1954

Securing the British Empire Games was a major coup for Vancouver and the Pacific National Exhibition. Initial plans called for the construction of a stadium at the University of British Columbia, but when that idea fell through Exhibition Park was offered as an alternative. To allow for construction of the stadium, the P.N.E. had to close down the golf course and a recently built driving range.

John Landy
3:59.6

Roger Bannister
3:58.8

British Empire Game Marathon, 1954

What the Landy–Bannister confrontation offered in excitement, the marathon more than matched in drama and tension. British runner Jim Peters was the first competitor to enter Empire Stadium, needing only to circle the track one time to claim victory. Virtually in a coma when he entered the stadium, Peters lurched and staggered 200 more yards towards his goal before he collapsed for the final time and was disqualified. Joe McGhee of Scotland won the race.

The Miracle Mile: Bannister–Landy, 1954

One of the greatest confrontations in sports history occurred in Empire Stadium during the 1954 British Empire Games. Roger Bannister, the first man to break the four–minute mile barrier, was being challenged by Australian Frank Landy. The memorable race, which saw Bannister pull away in the final stretch to win, was a fitting inauguration for the newest sports facility at Exhibition Park.

Canadian Professional Football, 1960

The opening of Empire Stadium in 1954 cleared the way for an expansion of sporting activities at Exhibition Park. Vancouver had long desired a Canadian Football league franchise and was finally rewarded when a team was granted in 1954. The largest facility of its type in Canada, Empire Stadium was the natural site for the Grey Cup game and that event was finally pried from its Eastern Canadian base in 1955.

Auto Show, 1958

As the P.N.E. facilities continued to expand, the directors cast around for new sources of revenue to finance and maintain the physical plant. The most notable change was the large increase in the number of such events as the Auto Show. The P.N.E. did not operate these attractions, but rather rented the necessary facilities to a promoter who was responsible for the presentation.

Aerial View of the Pacific National Exhibition, c. 1960

The 1950's saw some important physical changes at Exhibition Park. The golf course and recently erected driving range were gone and Happyland vacated its former home in the northwest corner of the grounds. A new exhibit facility, the B.C. Building, can be seen along Hastings Street, and next to it is the new site for the amusement complex and Empire Stadium.

6

Years of Challenge and Change, 1960–1982

The last twenty years have seen a continuation of several familiar themes in the history of the Pacific National Exhibition. The fair itself continued to undergo considerable change to keep current with changing public interests. Additions to the programme included such features as the Demolition Derby, the ever popular Timber Show and the Stadium Show/Star Spectacular which brought top–name Canadian and international performers to Vancouver during the fair.

As an institution, the P.N.E. underwent considerable change as well. As the 1960's opened, the association found itself embroiled in a major controversy with city council over the P.N.E.'s desire to build a sports arena at Exhibition Park. A compromise was worked out, resulting in the Agrodome, a building which in the end satisfied neither side in the dispute as it had limited utility as either an athletic facility or as an exhibit building. The P.N.E.'s next attempt to expand its physical plant met with less hostility and the resulting Pacific Coliseum was hailed as a major addition to Vancouver's entertainment and sporting facilities. The association, never a stranger to controversy, soon found itself immersed in yet another major battle in 1973. A conflict between a Boat Show and minor hockey over the use of the Forum spilled over into civic and provincial politics and when the dust had settled the old exhibition association had been forced to step aside and the B.C. Government assumed control of the exhibition.

On the surface, the 1973 take–over changed very little. The fair continued as before and year–round activities were expanded. As well, the P.N.E. continued to look to the future, planning for the further development of Exhibition Park and the annual fair. Several proposals, including a hotly debated concept called Multiplex, were brought forward, but as yet no major redevelopment has been undertaken by the recently founded administration.

An amazing variety of events including professional and amateur sports, religious meetings and trade shows continue to fill Vancouver's premier exhibition and sporting complex. As a focal point for local and provincial entertainment and recreation, and most importantly as the host of Western Canada's largest annual fair, the Pacific National Exhibition remains an integral part of the civic and provincial scene.

Timber Show, 1960

The first major timber show at the P.N.E. was staged as a
one-time event in 1960. Public response was very positive
and when a special attraction was needed for the 1966 fair it
was decided to resurrect the forestry competition. From that
point to the present, the Timber Show has been a popular
feature of the fair.

100

Chain Saw Race, 1966

Underhand Chopping, 1960's

Log Rolling, 1966

Willie the Whale, 1961

Beginning in 1959, the P.N.E. attempted to organize the fair around a central theme. The focus in 1961 was on a "Maritime Festival" and Willie the Whale was an important part of that feature. Inside the free attraction was an aquarium of tropical fish and a statue of King Neptune. The theme concept was eventually dropped as it proved to be too difficult to co-ordinate a variety of activities around a single idea.

P.N.E. Parade, 1960's and 1970's

While the basic content of the opening day parade, floats, bands, and clowns, has remained constant, each presentation has had a character all its own. Large crowds have continued to flock to downtown streets to view the spectacular.

Cassiar Rate Payers

"The PNE is continually encroaching on this district and commercializing it. They have developed it with complete disregard for the residential area.**"**

PNE Management

"Why is it when anyone comes forward with an idea which means progress they are immediately assailed by small–minded individuals who love to villify anything constructive.**"**

PNE General Manager Morrow.

Proposed New Brighton Beach Development, 1960

Aerial View of New Brighton Beach, 1960

As part of the 1961 Maritime Festival, the P.N.E. proposed to develop New Brighton Beach as a sight for boat races, a regatta and historical pageants. East end residents bitterly opposed the further development of one of the few parks in their area and they successfully thwarted the expansion plans. Importantly, this controversy marked the first significant conflict between the P.N.E. and local residents. Until this time, the east end had mainly provided staunch and consistent support for the fair, but in 1960-1961 relations began to strain.

Livestock Competition in the Agrodome, 1965

While the Agrodome was not particularly functional as an exhibit or athletic facility, it was a boon to the livestock competitions, offering an excellent venue for the events. Formerly restricted to small competition rings in the livestock buildings, the cattle judging and horse show events now moved to a large, and far more attractive facility. As a direct result, public interest in the various competitions increased.

Grand Champion, 1964

Demolition Derby

The type and variety of free entertainment offered at the fair is constantly changing. In the early 1970's, the PNE made a significant addition to their programme when they scheduled a daily "Demolition Derby" for the Outdoor Bowl to supplement the Timber Show which was also held in that spot. The new attraction proved particularly popular and became an annual exhibition feature.

Prize Homes, 1960's

The Prize Home remained a highlight of the annual exhibition, but the houses themselves varied greatly in design and popularity. Although experimental houses with unusual gimmicks often appeared over the years, most fairgoers preferred the traditional homes.

Prize Home, 1964

Prize Home, 1966

The PNE and the World "Outside"

❝ The Pacific National Exhibition seemed to be wearing the curious, if somewhat sombre crown of a mother–in–law of many years standing in a family indifferent to her many fine points but at the same time quite jealously possessive of her material assets. **❞**

Minutes of the Board of Directors, PNE, 19 September 1962.

B.C. International Trade Fair, 1961

As part of the 1958 Centennial, the B.C. government held an international trade fair designed to highlight the importance of the import and export trade to the provincial economy. Held afterwards on an irregular basis through the 1960's, the International Trade Fair provides yet another example of the growing diversity of activities at Exhibition Park.

Protestors at Entrance to P.N.E., 1968

Even the P.N.E. could not escape the heated political atmosphere of the 1960's. Under Regulation 25 of the P.N.E.'s rules and regulations, partisan political advertising was not allowed at the fair. When the association used this clause to prevent such groups as the Committee for Nuclear Disarmament and the People's Co–operative Bookstore from renting space they sparked a bitter dispute. Faced with prospect of picket lines throughout the exhibition, the P.N.E. relented.

Exhibition Park Racetrack
Racing has always been an important feature at Exhibition Park, and had actually preceded the development of an exhibition in the east Vancouver park. In 1960, the Ascot Jockey Club, tenants at Exhibition Park, merged operations with the B.C. Jockey Club, the operators of Lansdowne Park in Richmond. The merger left Exhibition Park as the site for all Lower Mainland thoroughbred racing and led to an expansion in the number of racing days and to the reconstruction of track facilities.

Johnny Longden and George Royal, 1965
George Royal was named Canadian Horse of the Year in 1965, when he won the B.C. Derby at the age of four. Jockey Johnny Longden began his career in 1927 and rode George Royal again in the last of his 6,000 victories in the San Juan Capistrano Handicap in 1966.

Construction of the Pacific Coliseum, 1967

After the embarrassment surrounding the Agrodome, the Pacific National Exhibition continued to formulate plans for the construction of a major sports arena at Exhibition Park. The association encountered some difficulty securing the required $6 million, but federal, provincial and civic funding was secured eventually and construction began in the winter of 1965–1966.

The Coliseum Completed, 1970's

Canucks First Goal in the Coliseum, against the Los Angeles Kings, 1970

Old Timers' Hockey Game, 1968

January 8, 1968 marked the official opening of the P.N.E.'s newest and most expensive facility, the Pacific Coliseum. To herald the occasion, the P.N.E. decided to stage an Old Timers' hockey game featuring former National Hockey League greats. Major league hockey did not follow as quickly as hoped, but an N.H.L. franchise was finally secured in 1969 and in the fall of 1970 the Vancouver Canucks skated onto Coliseum ice for the first time. Concerts, trade shows and other non–athletic events also took place in the 15,000–seat building.

Karen Magnussen, Canadian and World Champion Figure Skater, 1970's

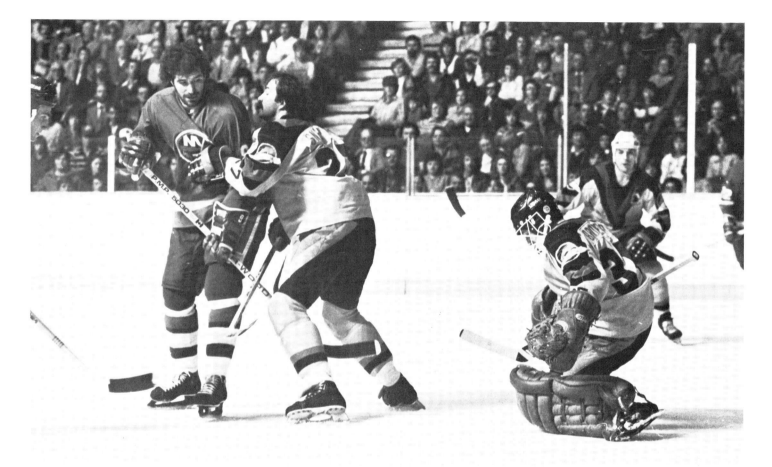

The Vancouver Canucks, 1982

The Canucks captured the hearts of Vancouverites when they reached the Stanley Cup Finals in May of 1982. Richard Brodeur's consistent goal tending earned him the nickname "King Richard" and assistant coach Roger Neilson's "white towel of surrender" became a symbol of support for the team. The hockey team played to capacity crowds in the Coliseum, and were hailed as heros, even after they lost to the reigning Stanley Cup champion New York Islanders in four games.

113

Boat Show, c. 1975

As the P.N.E. moved to make more productive use of their facilities on a year–round basis, trade shows proved to be particularly valuable tenants. The Auto Show, Home Show, Boat Show and others were usually staged annually and attracted large crowds to Exhibition Park. The P.N.E. had the only set of facilities in Vancouver capable of handling such events.

As a special feature in the 1967 Vancouver Boat Show, the promoters brought in "Walter", a killer whale, and placed him in a pool for the duration of the event. When the Boat Show was over, the whale was sold to the Vancouver Aquarium Society. Renamed "Skana", the whale was a much admired and beloved addition to the Aquarium, quickly becoming a fixture in the city.

Boat Show Clowns, 1966

Sports in Empire Stadium

Sporting events continued to draw large crowds to the P.N.E. grounds. The Vancouver Whitecaps, members of the North American Soccer League, played their first game in 1974, and won the prestigious Soccer Bowl in 1979, beating the Tampa Bay Rowdies. The B.C. Lions, principal tenants of Empire Stadium, continued their operations, and with the shift to interlocking schedules, held more home games.

115

The P.N.E. in 1973: A Political "Football"

February 22, 1973
Hon. Mr. Williams (NDP):

"We could make the exhibition grounds more significant for the province and more worthwhile for the people of the east side of the city.

Too often the PNE is simply a burden on the people of the east side of town. They have to live with the traffic problems almost daily as a result of that development. They have to deal daily with the mammoth invasion or intrusion into their residential neighbourhoods. I know that that can't be washed away, but it would be easier to take if the PNE were more responsive to their own needs right in the community.

The board of directors has continued to destroy the amenity qualities of the lands in the Pacific National Exhibition grounds. They used to be a pleasant place to be. They are no longer. We lost the golf course when there was a golf course in the ravine. We lost Callister Park for a long time to drag racing on what was the most important soccer pitch in the city for many years . . .

The Hon. Member for Langley (Mr. McClelland) said in a release the other day, 'Good Heavens! The Minister of Resources and the Attorney General want to turn the PNE into a giant community centre. Wouldn't that be a disaster?' You bet your sweet bippy we want to change it into a giant community centre."

Mr. McClelland (Social Credit): "I understand that the Pacific National Exhibition Board of Directors has resigned en masse today and has voted to turn the assets over to the City of Vancouver. Mr. Chairman, The implications of this for the agricultural community in British Columbia are staggering — simply staggering, Mr. Chairman. I must say that I can understand the frustrations that this board must have felt after getting a hatchet job from this Government, and particularly from a Minister of this Government.**"**

Debates of the Legislative Assembly, Province of British Columbia re: Take–over of the Pacific National Exhibition (excerpts).

116

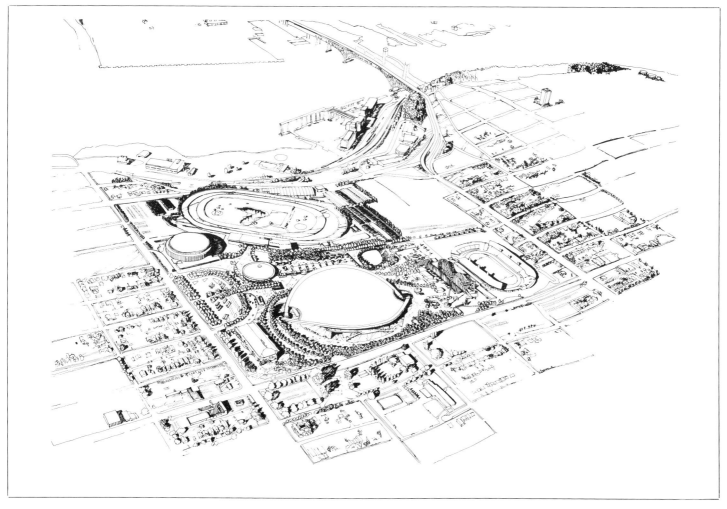

Multiplex Plan, 1977

When engineering studies suggested that Empire Stadium had but a few years left as a viable sports facility, the P.N.E. formulated plans for the construction of a new stadium. The proposed 60,000 seat stadium, designed to incorporate exhibit facilities into the structure, lost out to a counter proposal for a stadium to be built in downtown Vancouver.

Midway
One of the greatest attractions of the exhibition is the fair itself, the hustle and bustle of the fairgoers, the smells of the food stands, the fervent calls of the carnival operators, the screams of the young children on the midway rides and the seemingly endless array of sights and sounds which assault the senses the moment one enters the grounds. To the people of Vancouver, the fair is an institution that is at once familiar and nostalgic.

118

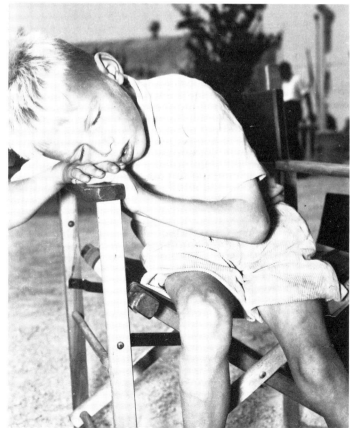

Faces of the P.N.E.

The essence of the fair, beyond midways, displays and attractions, is people. The Exhibition is, above all else, a people place, a place for screaming kids on rides, youngsters tired out from a long day at the fairgrounds, sticky faces and cotton candy, arms wrapped around a midway prize and family fun. Such are the truly enduring images, and the indelible memories, of the Pacific National Exhibition.

The Pacific National Exhibition, 1982

This aerial shot shows the P.N.E. as it is today. The two major projects of the 1960's, the Agrodome and the Pacific Coliseum, are in place. Both the exhibition and the Greater Vancouver area have undergone massive changes since the first fair was held in heavily forested Hastings Park in 1910. Vancouver in 1982 seemed to prove that the boosters associated with the first exhibition had been right, for their city had grown to be one of North America's great centres.

Vancouver's Fair

The visual moments preserved by photographs presented here reveal 'the fair' as it has been known to three generations of Vancouverites. These individual glimpses taken together however, disclose much more than just Sir Wilfrid Laurier's arrival at the fair in 1910, the display of the Begg Motor Co. Ltd. in 1919, the Livestock Competition in 1930 or the Miss PNE Contestants in 1954. In their collectivity, the pictures tell us that Vancouver's fair was not simply an annual summer's amusement. The development of the fair and its changing character over time, so clearly revealed in these pictures, reflect the transformation of the city and community of which it has been an integral part. The fair, in essence, is an image of its setting, providing a glimpse of life style and basic values, of how people viewed themselves and their region, of what they felt they had accomplished and what they would wish to be their future. Not just in Vancouver, the exhibition was of Vancouver.

Photographic Credits

H. R. H. PRINCE PHILIP, DUKE OF EDINBURGH
IN ATTENDANCE AT BRITISH EMPIRE AND COMMONWEALTH GAMES

Oceans of fun in '61

AUG. 19
TO
SEPT. 4
(EXCEPT SUNDAYS)

IT'S MARINE FESTIVAL YEAR AT THE

PACIFIC
NATIONAL
EXHIBITION

VANCOUVER, CANADA